THE
WILD PIGS

BY
MARK E. AHLSTROM

*For Art, so that he never
forgets returning from
his first wild hog hunt.*

EDITED BY
DR. HOWARD SCHROEDER

**Professor in Reading and Language Arts
Dept. of Elementary Education
Mankato State University**

**PRODUCED AND DESIGNED BY
BAKER STREET PRODUCTIONS
Mankato, MN**

CRESTWOOD HOUSE
Mankato, Minnesota

LIBRARY OF CONGRESS CATALOGING IN PUBLICATION DATA

Ahlstrom, Mark E.
  The wild pigs.

  (Wildlife, habits & habitat)
  SUMMARY: Examines three kinds of North American wild pigs, their physical characteristics, habitats, behavior, and enemies.
  1. Suidae--Juvenile literature. 2. Swine--Juvenile literature. (1. Pigs) I. Schroeder, Howard. II. Baker Street Productions. III. Title. IV. Series.
QL737.U58A37   1986   599.73'4   86-2282
ISBN 0-89686-272-0 (lib. bdg.)

<table>
International Standard Book Number:
Library Binding 0-89686-272-0

Library of Congress Catalog Card Number:
86-2282
</table>

ILLUSTRATION CREDITS:

Leonard Lee Rue III: 5, 16-17, 19, 23, 30
Phil & Loretta Hermann: 7, 10, 27, 36
Stephen J. Krasemann/DRK Photo: 13, 24-25
Irene Vandermolen/Leonard Lee Rue Enterprises: 15
Gary Milburn/Tom Stack & Assoc.: 20
Warren & Genny Garst/Tom Stack & Assoc.: 33
Fiona Sunquist/Tom Stack & Assoc.: 39
Kenneth W. Fink: 43

CRESTWOOD HOUSE

Hwy. 66 South, Box 3427
Mankato, MN 56002-3427

TABLE OF CONTENTS

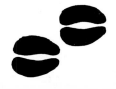

"That takes the cake!"

As the sky started to get light in the east, everything seemed normal. For Ken Fuller, it looked like a good day to be deer hunting.

It was November 16, 1985, the opening day of the second deer hunting season in southern Minnesota. Ken had gotten up long before daylight. He picked up two friends and drove a few miles north of the city of St. Peter.

When the men entered the woods, it was still dark. They split up and headed for the tree stands that they had built earlier in the year. Their "stands" were small wooden platforms, located in trees along a hillside that faced the Minnesota River Valley.

Ken climbed into his stand and got ready. He was getting excited as he loaded his shotgun with slugs. He thought his chances of seeing deer were very good. The whitetail deer in the area would be in the middle of the "rut," and it was cold. This usually meant that the deer would be active during daylight hours.

As soon as it got light enough to see, Ken began to check out the woods around his stand. He was looking for the brown shape of a deer sneaking through the woods. He hoped one would come close enough for a shot.

Ken spotted some movement out of the corner of his eye, and turned to look. He was not ready for what he saw.

At first, he refused to believe his eyes. He saw a large black animal, with short legs. Ken had hunted for years, and had never seen anything like this animal. Even in the dim light of early morning, he knew it wasn't a deer. Deer are brown and have long legs.

Ken knew better than to shoot something he wasn't sure of, so he just watched the animal. Before long, it was right under his tree stand. After awhile, it wandered away.

"It looked like a pig, except it didn't look like a pig," Ken explained to his friends when they came by later.

"It looked like a pig, except it didn't look like a pig."

"Yeah, sure," his friends said when they saw the tracks made by the animal. The tracks looked like deer tracks. Ken's friends thought he had a case of "buck fever"—that he had been so excited about seeing a deer he forgot to shoot. It's something that happens more often than most hunters will admit. The more Ken tried to explain the animal, the more his friends teased him.

As they walked out of the woods, they met Tom Merkley. Tom lived nearby and is a taxidermist. Because he deals with animals all the time, Tom listened to Ken's story with great interest. Tom told Ken that he had seen a wild hog of some kind. Tom also added that he was more than a little surprised. He had never heard of wild hogs running free anywhere close to Minnesota.

Ken and his friends decided to shoot the animal if they got another chance. They now knew that the wild hog would be a rare trophy for a Minnesota hunter. Ken, of course, was the most eager to get another chance. He hoped to prove to his friends that he had not been seeing things!

Luck was with Ken. As they were walking through the woods, he spotted the animal from about seventy yards away. Ken took a shot.

"It ran around in a circle like it was real mad, and then ran into a bunch of trees," Ken said later. Because Tom had warned them that a wounded wild hog might attack, the men were careful.

When wild hogs walk on soft ground, they make tracks that look like deer tracks.

As they got close to the clump of trees, the hog jumped out, snorting as it came. Ken shot again, hitting the hog in the head. This time the animal went down, and stayed down.

Ken got a surprise when he took a close look at the dead animal. He found where he had hit the hog with his first shot. It was in the neck and shoulder area. On most other animals, such a shot would have been fatal. "You won't believe it, but all there was was a big 'goose egg' bump. The slug just bounced off!"

Later, the men decided to report what had happened to the Minnesota Department of Natural Resources. After hearing the story, Roger Holmes, chief of the Wildlife Section, could only say, "That takes the cake!" He had never heard of a true wild hog being seen in the wild in Minnesota.

And that is what the animal turned out to be. The local experts think that it was a European wild hog. Their best guess is that it escaped from a shooting preserve or game farm **somewhere** nearby. The experts aren't sure where "somewhere" might be.

Ken Fuller doesn't care. He had the four hundred pound (182 k) wild hog butchered. He truly "brought home the bacon!" He's also having Tom mount the head, so he can share the hunt with friends for years to come.

— M.E.A.

CHAPTER ONE:

How many are there?

Before we take a closer look at the wild pigs found in North America, we need to get some things straight. It wasn't easy trying to decide which animals to include in this book. The problem is that the experts can't seem to agree on which animals can be called North American wild pigs.

One expert said, in effect, that there were no wild pigs in North America. The reason given was that the members of the pig family that do live here were not native to North America. This would exclude even the European wild hog, because it was imported from Europe. It also excludes the peccary, because it is not an official member of the pig family.

Another expert said that the peccary was the only North American wild pig. This expert didn't think it was important that the peccary wasn't in the pig family. It was good enough that this North American native was "pig-like" in its day-to-day actions.

A third expert included only the peccary and the feral pig. The feral pig is a domestic pig that has returned to the wild. This expert thought that the feral pig should be considered a native. Why? Because feral pigs have

The collared peccary is the only wild pig that is a native of North America.

been running wild for several hundred years in some parts of North America. The European wild hog was not included because it was no longer "pure." The expert said that the European hogs had bred with feral pigs over the years. He thought that the offspring of such crossbreeding should be called feral pigs.

Yet another expert said that the offspring of European hogs and feral pigs should be thought of as a separate kind of North American wild pig. This expert called it a European hog-feral pig hybrid. This expert also excluded the European wild hog. The expert gave the same reason as the third expert—the European import was no longer pure.

A fifth expert could not bring himself to even think of the feral pig as a wild animal. As far as he was concerned, they were plain-old pigs that had gone a little wild. This same expert said that the offspring of European hogs and feral pigs should be called European wild hogs. He said that the offspring looked and behaved very much like the pure European hog.

Getting practical

I could go on-and-on, but I think you get the point. It's hopeless to be "correct" about which animals to include in a book on the wild pigs of North America. Instead, I've decided to be practical.

I've included the peccary in this book because it's thought of as a wild pig in the areas where it lives. Even though biologists don't put it in the pig family, it does behave very much like a pig.

The feral pig is included because it has been able to exist in the wild without any help from people. It is also thought of as a wild pig in the areas where it lives.

Lastly, I settled on the European wild hog. It's true that there are few, if any, pure European hogs left in North America. It's also true that these hogs have bred with feral pigs in most areas of the hogs' range. But

I agree with what the fifth expert said. The offspring continue to behave and look much like their pure European cousins. I'll also admit that I like the name. Wild hog is much more "fun" than European wild hog-feral pig hybrid!

Choosing the right names

There is one last thing before we proceed. We need to agree on the names to be used for the animals in this book. Again, I've decided to be practical.

There are two kinds of peccaries that exist in the world. One, the white-lipped peccary, lives only in South America. The other, the collared peccary, lives in both North and South America. It's the collared peccary that is described in this book. You might also know this animal as either a musk hog or a javelina. (Javelina is from the Spanish word for "spear," *javeline*, which no doubt refers to the animal's tusks.) In this book, peccary, a short version of the proper name, will be used for this wild pig.

The European wild hog has gone by several names. Where it lives in the eastern United States, it is often called the razorback. It's also commonly been called

In the eastern United States, wild hogs are often called "razorbacks."

the wild boar, even by biologists. Lately, however, the experts have fixed the mistake. They realized that people were getting confused. Because "boar" is the name for a male pig, they changed the name of this animal to European wild hog. That covered both sexes. In this book, a short version of the proper name will again be used. From now on, the term wild hog, will be used to describe this wild pig.

The domestic pig that has returned to the wild is often called either a wild pig or a wild hog by many people. The experts attach another word, "feral." Feral just means untamed or wild. To biologists, this animal has been either a feral hog or a feral pig. To be both proper, and to avoid confusing this animal with the wild hog, the term feral pig, will be used in this book.

So, there you have it. Hopefully, we'll now understand each other at least a little bit better as we take a closer look at the wild pigs of North America.

Even-toed ungulates

All three North American wild pigs belong to a large group of mammals called "even-toed ungulates" by biologists. These hooved animals bear their weight on an even number of toes when they walk. This group,

Wild pigs walk on an even number of toes.

whose scientific name is the order *Artiodactyla*, contains about one-tenth of the earth's land mammals. One writer joked that belonging to this order was about as important as having your name in the New York City telephone book! Animals as different as deer, hippos, bison, camels, giraffes, cows, and sheep are all included.

Most of the animals in this large order belong to a suborder called the ruminants. Ruminants are animals that eat plants and chew a cud. North American wild pigs belong to a much smaller suborder called the non-ruminants. The animals in this group are omnivorous,

A peccary looks for food near a waterhole.

which means that they eat both plants and flesh.

The non-ruminant group includes all kinds of pigs (domestic and wild), the two kinds of peccaries, and the two kinds of hippos. All of the animals in this suborder have canine teeth that are enlarged into tusks. The tusks are used to get food and as weapons for fighting. The non-ruminants are all very good fighters. Because of this, they have very few natural enemies.

Now that you know how the three kinds of North American wild pigs fit into nature's order, it's time to take a closer look at each of the animals.

CHAPTER TWO:

A big family

There are eight species, or kinds, of wild pigs found in the world. They live all across Europe, Asia, and Africa. Biologists call this group of mammals the Old World Pigs.

The species with the biggest range is the wild hog. The scientific name for this species is *Sus scrofa*. This wild pig is found all over the southern parts of Europe and Asia, from Ireland to Japan. It is also found along the north coast of Africa. It is thought that these wild hogs were used to breed the first domestic pigs. In fact, biologists use the same name, *Sus scrofa*, for domestic pigs.

A smart game animal

People have been hunting the wild hog for a very long time. In many areas it was the main source of meat. Cave paintings that are known to be thousands of years old show hunts for wild hogs. The Greeks and Romans made great sport of hunting the wild pigs with spears.

Wild hogs are still hunted all across their range for food and sport. It may surprise you to know that they are thought of as one of the most dangerous animals to hunt. Many hunters think they are more dangerous than a tiger. When cornered or wounded they will attack. A wild hog can bite more savagely than bears, lions, or tigers. Only the killer whale, of all mammals on earth, can inflict a worse bite. The hogs can also slash with their tusks, causing serious wounds. Wild hogs have been known to attack and gore everything from tigers to horses to elephants!

You might think that Old Fido, the family dog, is quite smart. You would be correct to say that dogs are smarter than pet cats, but so are rabbits, birds, goats, and rats. Compared to a pig (of any kind) Old Fido is dumb. Experts place wild hogs right behind the large apes when it comes to brain power. The apes are thought to be the smartest animals on earth.

Wild hogs are very smart animals, and get along well with each other.

Because of their tusks, large wild hogs can be very dangerous.

Because wild hogs are so smart, they are not easy to hunt. Because the animals are also dangerous, there is always a chance that the hunter will become the hunted. It is mainly for these two reasons that wild hogs have been popular game animals over the years.

Wild hogs come to America

Austin Corbin brought the first wild hogs to North America in 1893. He brought in fifty hogs from the Black Forest of Germany. Mr. Corbin released the wild hogs on his private game preserve in the Blue Mountains of New Hampshire. Over the years, a number of the hogs escaped from the preserve. They were able to survive on their own, and a small number of wild hogs still live there.

Fifteen to twenty more wild hogs from Germany were released in the Adirondack Mountains of New York in 1900. Despite hunting, this herd was able to maintain itself for almost twenty years. By 1920, however, the last one had been killed.

In 1910, George Moore decided to build a game preserve on Hooper Bald. Hooper Bald is in the Great Smoky Mountains in western North Carolina. Mr. Moore built the preserve to entertain business clients. He wanted to provide his clients with some unusual hunting. In addition to elk, bison, and mule deer, he decided to bring in some wild hogs from Europe.

Fourteen wild hogs were released on Hooper Bald in 1912. Moore had built a fence around a five hundred acre (202 ha) plot to contain the hogs. He also hired a game manager, Garland McGuire, to watch over all the animals. Over the years, the hogs did very well. Even though they were hunted all the time, they increased in number.

In 1920, McGuire decided that he wanted to get rid of the sixty hogs that were inside the fence. He felt that they had become more trouble than they were worth. He had better uses in mind for the five hundred acres, so he set up a one-day hunt for his friends. He planned to surround the hogs, slowly forcing them into a smaller and smaller area. He thought it would then be easy to shoot the animals.

On the day of the hunt, all went as planned for awhile. The hunters and their dogs squeezed the wild hogs into a small area of the pen. Then the hogs attacked! Most of the hunters ran for their lives. When it was all over, there were twelve dead dogs and two dead hogs. The rest of the wild hogs broke through the fence and escaped.

The rest, as they say, is history. The wild hogs found the Great Smoky Mountains much to their liking. The habitat was perfect. They soon expanded their range into the neighboring states of Tennessee, Kentucky, and West Virginia.

Slender and strong

The wild hog is not fat like its domestic relative. Because it has to move about to find food, and run to escape its enemies, the wild hog stays thin. It also grows strong muscles. An adult boar, or male hog, is usually about thirty inches (77 cm) tall at the shoulder. Most boars are between four and five feet (1.2 - 1.5 m) long, and weigh up to 350 pounds (159 kg). Female hogs, or sows, are usually smaller than the males.

The wild hog is smaller than the domestic hog.

Female wild hogs (left) are usually smaller than the males (right).

Most wild hogs are dark brown or jet black in color. Some hogs, however, have a frosting of white on the ends of their guard hairs. These hogs appear to be gray in color. The guard hairs are stiff, almost like the bristles on a brush. There is a layer of short, soft hair beneath the long guard hairs. This thick layer of hair keeps the hogs warm in cold weather. Many wild hogs have extra long hairs on their necks and shoulders, forming what looks like a mane.

The hog's head is cone-shaped, and ends in a flexible snout. The hairless snout is round and formed of cartilage. Hogs use their snouts to root, or dig, for food. The eyes are quite small. Guard hairs on the hog's face make the eyes look even smaller than they really are. Unlike the floppy ears of the domestic pig, wild hogs always have their ears erect. The ears are usually about five inches (13 cm) long. A hog's tail is quite long, and has a tuft of hair on its tip.

Tusks and shields

The wild boar is probably best known for its tusks. The tusks are really enlarged canine teeth. Both the upper and lower canine teeth are curved backward and outward. Friction between the upper and lower canines makes the lower canines razor sharp! The tusks keep

Tusks are used to dig for food and as weapons for fighting. They are razor sharp!

growing as long as the hogs live. Most hogs have tusks that are several inches long, and they've been known to grow to a length of nine inches (23 cm). Tusks are used to dig for food.

Boars usually have the longest tusks, which they use to fight each other during the rutting season. The fights are often bloody, but seldom fatal to either boar. If the boars did not have special protection, one of them would surely die. The boars are protected by a special shield that grows before the rutting season each year. This plate of tissue grows on each side of the boar, from the shoulder to the last rib. The shield is about one inch (2.5 cm) thick, and is made of keratin. It is quite rigid, and can be seen moving under the boar's skin as it walks.

It would be a good guess that this shield is what caused the shotgun slug to "bounce off" the wild hog in the Introduction. If the shield can stop a shotgun slug, imagine how strong it must be! It would also be a good guess that the hog was a boar. Females do not grow this shield.

Home range is varied

In addition to the areas already mentioned, there is only one other place that wild hogs live in good numbers in North America. This is on Santa Cruz Island off the California coast. In all areas of its range, the wild hogs live in a forest habitat.

The size of a hog's home range varies by sex and with the seasons. Old boars often travel by themselves and have the largest home ranges. Sows with young usually have the smallest home ranges. During the fall, hogs may walk several miles to locate their favorite food, which is acorns. During the winter, deep snow may keep them from moving about. At this time of the year, their home range may be as small as a square mile (2.5 sq. k).

Wild hogs move about their range in herds as large as fifty animals. Females and their young travel together. The males are alone, or in a separate group. The boars are only with the sows during the rutting season.

While moving through their range, hogs usually walk or trot. However, when it has to get away from danger, a hog can run almost as fast as a deer! The hog's feet equip it to move well on different kinds of ground. There are four "toes" on each foot. The two middle toes form narrow hooves, which give hogs a good grip on hard ground. The two outside toes are "dewclaws," which are smaller hooves on the back of each foot. When the ground is soft, the dewclaws help support the hog's weight. Water doesn't stop wild hogs either— they are very good swimmers.

"Dew claws" are the smaller hooves on the back of each foot.

Food and feeding habits

Wild hogs are most active during the daylight. Most of their waking hours are spent either eating or looking for food. They usually feed early in the morning, and again late in the afternoon. In between feeding times, they rest or sleep.

As was said earlier, wild hogs are omnivorous. They will eat almost anything. The prefer various roots and tubers, which they dig out of the ground with their snouts. They tear up large areas while looking for these foods. This habit sometimes gets them in trouble with foresters, who say that the hogs kill too many small trees.

The hogs also eat many kinds of grasses and fruits. And they never turn down meat, dead or alive. They have been known to eat rodents, birds, frogs, grasshoppers, fish, crabs, worms, and snakes. They have no trouble killing the rattlesnakes found in their range. The hogs seem to be immune to the snakes' poison. They kill the snakes by jumping upon them again and again.

During the fall, they are attracted to nuts of all kinds. In addition to acorns, they search for beechnuts, pecans, and hickory nuts. When the first snows of winter cover their supply of nuts, the hogs move to marsh and swamp areas. The ground in these areas usually stays soft, and the wild hogs can dig for roots all through the winter. To help keep warm during the winter, wild hogs often sleep on top of each other in a pile!

Senses and sounds

Wild hogs depend most on their sense of smell. They find all of their food, even that which is underground, by using their noses. It's no wonder, then, that their sense of smell is very good. Their sense of hearing is also quite good. They use their rather large, erect ears to detect danger at a distance. Their sense of smell is used to detect danger that doesn't make noise—like a hiding or sneaking predator. Because wild hogs usually live in areas that are thick with trees and plants, they cannot rely on their eyes to warn them of danger. Their vision is poor.

Like most wild animals, wild hogs communicate with each other by making sounds. To warn the herd of danger, or when scared, hogs squeal. Grunts let herd members know where each other is. Sows give "orders" to their piglets, or young, with a number of soft grunting sounds.

Rutting and raising the young

Both males and females are able to breed by the time they are a year old. Whether they do or not depends on the supply of food. If the supply is good, the young hogs will mate. Almost none of the young hogs will mate if food is in short supply.

Although wild hogs can breed at any time during the

year, most of the rutting takes place during December. During the rut, boars fight with each other for the right to breed with the sows in their home range. The larger, stronger boars usually do most of the breeding.

The gestation period is usually about 115 days. Just before giving birth, a sow separates herself from the herd. She usually builds a nest with small branches and grass. From three to twelve piglets may be born. The older sows have the most piglets. The piglets are born with very little hair, and must be kept warm.

After about a week, if the weather is warm, the piglets leave the nest and learn to look for food. Although they will nurse for three months, they start to eat solid food after two weeks. For the first six months the piglets have a striped coat to help them hide from danger. By fall, the young hogs get a new adult-looking coat of hair. The young usually stay with their mother until she gives birth again in the spring.

The piglets have a striped coat.

33

The biggest enemy?

During the fifteen to twenty years that a hog will live in the wild, it faces very few enemies. A large black bear is the only predator that might take on an adult wild hog. Young hogs are killed by bears, bobcats, and foxes. While people hunt wild hogs, it's most often done to control the number of hogs living in a certain area. By preventing an overpopulation, hunting serves the purpose of keeping a herd healthy.

The biggest "enemy" of the wild hog is a lack of suitable habitat. The areas where they live cannot support any more hogs. At present there are about five thousand wild hogs in North America. The only way to increase their number is to transplant them to new areas. That kind of effort takes time and a lot of money. And the experts have to be very careful about where they might move the animals. The future of wild hogs in North America is assured, it's just a question of how many there will be.

CHAPTER THREE:

The first pigs in North America

Many of the early explorers to North America brought domestic pigs with them. DeSoto brought pigs to Florida in 1593. Other Spanish explorers brought pigs to California in 1769. Captain Cook had pigs with him when he came to the Hawaiian Islands in 1778. The pigs were brought along so the explorers would have a supply of meat in the New World.

Before long, many of the pigs escaped from their pens in the settlements. The climate was mild where all these settlements were found, and there was plenty of natural food. The free-roaming pigs adapted to their new habitat, and became feral, or wild.

As the years passed, the feral pigs expanded their range. Florida's feral pigs moved north and east along the coastlines. Today, feral pigs live in coastal areas as far north as Virginia, and as far west as Texas. In California, feral pigs are now found in the coastal mountains from Mendocino to Santa Barbara. They are also found in the foothills along many parts of the Central Valley. In Hawaii, there are feral pigs on the islands of Hawaii, Maui, Molokai, Oahu, and Kauai.

There are also small numbers of feral pigs in Arizona,

Some feral pigs look very much like their wild hog relatives.

Oklahoma, and Arkansas. No doubt other areas have at least a few feral pigs, too. Wherever domestic pigs are raised in mild climates, they can survive in the wild.

Smaller than domestic pigs

Two main changes occur to domestic pigs when they become wild. Feral pigs get smaller and their coats of hair get coarser and thicker. These changes are caused by the conditions in which they live. Feral pigs get smaller, and thinner, because they have to work to find food. They grow heavier coats because they need the added protection. The longer a population of feral pigs has been living in the wild, the smaller they become.

Most feral pig boars weigh from 135 to 235 pounds (61 - 106 k), and are from four to six feet (1.2 - 1.8 m) long. They are about thirty inches (77 cm) tall at the shoulder. Sows are usually about one-fourth smaller than boars.

Other changes

In general, feral pigs look like a cross between domestic pigs and wild hogs. They are thinner than domestic pigs, but fatter than wild hogs. Some are spotted black and brown or black and white, like many domestic pigs. Others are dark brown, or even black, like wild hogs. Feral pigs have tusks that are longer than a farmer's pigs, but shorter than a wild hog's tusks.

Many years ago, some wild hogs were transplanted from the great Smoky Mountains to California. Feral pigs have bred with the wild hogs through the years. The result has been that feral hogs in California look much like their wild hog relatives. In areas where domestic pigs regularly escape, feral pigs look more like their domestic relatives.

Behavior is in between, too

The longer a feral hog herd has lived in the wild, the more it behaves like a wild hog herd. Their home range gets larger. The boars become more aggressive and dangerous. The sows give birth to fewer piglets. In short, they slowly adjust to living on their own in the wild.

Feral pigs soon learn to root for food in the ground, and before long are eating the same foods as wild hogs. Their senses become keener, and they are better able to defend themselves from predators. Feral pigs have more large predators in their range than wild hogs do. Alligators, black bears, bobcats, mountain lions, and coyotes all prey on feral pigs. As with wild hogs, the younger feral pigs are in the most danger from predators.

Disease is a very big problem for the feral pigs. Unlike wild hogs, who suffer from few diseases, feral pigs are affected by many diseases and parasites. Because of this problem, very few feral pigs live for more than three years.

Too many feral pigs?

It is not known how many feral pigs are living on their ranges in North America. Until the 1960's, no one cared.

That all changed when damage caused by feral pigs began to be noticed. Forest managers noticed that the pigs' rooting was beginning to kill a lot of young trees. Their rooting was also causing erosion problems along streams and road banks. In an effort to control the number of pigs, people were encouraged to hunt feral pigs.

At present, about one hundred thousand feral pigs are killed each year by hunters. In spite of the hunting, the pigs continue to be a problem in many areas. This means that feral pigs are able to quickly replace themselves. It would appear that these domestic-pigs-gone-wild have a firm footing in North America.

Feral pigs can reproduce quickly in their rich habitat.

CHAPTER FOUR:

The little pig

The collared peccary, known as *Dicotyles tajacu* by biologists, is North America's only native wild pig. This little pig had some huge ancestors. The fossil remains of one of its ancients has a skull that alone measures three feet (.9 m) long!

The entire body of today's peccary seldom measures over three feet (.9 m) in length. They stand between eighteen and twenty-two inches (46 - 56 cm) tall at the shoulder, and weigh from thirty to sixty pounds (14 - 27 k). Adult males and females in the same herd are about the same size.

The peccary looks much like a smaller version of a wild hog. It has a long snout, which it also uses for rooting, and small eyes on a cone-shaped head. Its pointed ears are held erect. Its coarse hair is a "salt-and-pepper" gray color, and the hair on its neck can be erected into a mane. It gets its name from the white "collar" that runs around its neck.

Unlike the wild hog, the peccary's tail is very short. It has a pair of hooves and a pair of dewclaws on each front foot. However, its black feet have only three "toes"—a pair of hooves and a single dewclaw. The peccary's tusks are also different from those on a wild hog. The tusks on a peccary are straight rather than curved. Both the upper and lower canine teeth are enlarged into tusks that are about two inches (5.1 cm) long. The tusks are razor sharp.

A large range

The peccary's range begins in the southern parts of Texas, Arizona, and New Mexico in the United States. The range then extends southward across Mexico, Central America, and into South America. Throughout most of its range in North America, the peccary lives in dry, brushy areas or scrub oak forests. They are omnivorous, like wild hogs and feral pigs.

Prickly pears are one of their favorite foods. This is probably because prickly pears have a great deal of moisture in them. Prickly pears, and other "succulents," or plants that contain moisture, are often the only source of water in the peccary's dry habitat. Peccaries dig into the ground to find roots and tubers. They eat fruits, berries, and nuts of all kinds. Insects, birds' eggs, and reptiles are also part of their diet. Like other wild pigs, peccaries also eat snakes. It is said that a herd of peccaries can clear an area of rattlesnakes!

A small home range

Most peccaries live in a home range that is only one to two miles square (2.6 - 5.2 sq. k). They use regular paths to get about their home range. Peccaries travel in herds that number from six to thirty animals. Males, females, and the young are in the same herd.

During the hot summer months, peccaries feed only in the early morning and in the evening. During the day, they dig holes beneath brush or trees and lie in the shade. During the winter months, they usually eat all day long. If peccaries find a cave in their territory, they will use it. A cave keeps them cool during the summer and warm during the winter.

Peccaries can move quickly when they have to do so. They can "swap ends" in an instant, and can broad jump six feet (1.8 m) from a standing position. They can run away at speeds of up to twenty-five miles per hour (40 k per hour). Like other wild pigs, they are good swimmers.

Senses & sounds

Experts say that the peccary can smell food that is six inches (15 cm) deep in the ground. Its sense of hearing is also very good. Because their vision is poor, peccaries depend on avoiding predators by hearing them at a distance.

While active, members of the herd grunt constantly. This serves to keep the herd in touch. A barking cough is used to warn the herd of danger. Peccaries squeal if they are startled or injured.

Peccaries have a scent gland on their backs. The strong odor given off by the gland is why the peccary is often called a musk hog. The odor smells much like a skunk's. Peccaries rub the gland on rocks and bushes to mark their home range. They also release the scent to warn other herd members of danger.

Mating and raising the young

Both males and females are able to mate before they are one year old. Most females will mate at an early age. However, the strongest male will mate with almost all of the females in a herd. There are often some mean fights among the largest males in the herd for the right to breed with the females.

Although peccaries can mate at any time, most breeding takes place in February and March. Most young are born in July and August, after a gestation period of 145 days. Usually there are two young in a litter.

Peccary females usually have two piglets in a litter.

Sometimes three or four young are born. Females usually give birth in a protected area, like a cave or a thick clump of brush.

A few hours after being born, the young are able to get up and follow their mother. The young are the size of baby rabbits. Their reddish-brown coats have a single black stripe down their backs. The female stands while the young nurse. After a couple of days, the female rejoins the herd with her young.

Enemies

The average peccary lives for six or seven years in the wild. Some may live for twelve or fifteen years. A female peccary in the New York Zoo lived to be twenty-five years old.

During its time in the wild, the peccary's most feared enemy is the jaguar. These large cats can easily kill a peccary. Luckily for the peccary, there are not too many jaguars prowling their range! Coyotes, foxes, and ocelots prey on young peccaries, but they cannot kill an adult.

As is often the case, people's actions cause the most harm. In the case of the peccary, it's the loss of habitat. More and more land is being cleared of brush and made into pasture for livestock. When brushy cover is removed, the peccary cannot survive. While the peccary is in no danger of becoming extinct, their numbers are getting smaller each year.

MAP:

☐ Most feral pigs in North America
live within the these areas.

☐ Most wild hogs in North America
live within these areas.

▨ Most peccaries in North America
live within these areas.

INDEX/GLOSSARY:

INDEX/GLOSSARY:

WILDLIFE
HABITS & HABITAT

READ AND ENJOY THE SERIES:

If you would like to know more about all kinds of wildlife, you should take a look at the other books in this series.

You'll find books on bald eagles and other birds. Books on alligators and other reptiles. There are books about deer and other big-game animals. And there are books about sharks and other creatures that live in the ocean.

In all of the books you will learn that life in the wild is not easy. But you will also learn what people can do to help wildlife survive. So read on!